G. AI

30-days of prayer • 30-days of prayer • 30-days of prayer • 30-days of prayer • 30-days of prayer

let's pray

Intend
PUBLISHING

© 2016 by G. Allen Jackson
ISBN 978-1-61718-039-2

Published by Intend Publishing
Murfreesboro, Tennessee

Unless otherwise noted Scripture references are from the Holy Bible, New International Version®. Copyright © 1973, 1978, 1984 International Bible Society. Used by permission of Zondervan. All rights reserved.

Cover Design by Kim Russell / Wahoo Designs
Page Layout by Bart Dawson

Printed in the United States of America

1 2 3 4 5—CHG—20 19 18 17 16

TABLE OF CONTENTS

INTRODUCTION

LET'S PRAY

Our words hold authority. With the words we choose we can bring joy or inflict pain. When we make the effort to offer prayers to God, we are transformed. Prayer lifts our lives above the gravitational pull of the ordinary and opens our lives to the eternal purposes of God.

This simple book is intended to provide a bit of momentum to our emerging prayer life. Use the prayers each day for a month. With an investment of a few minutes, a new response to life can take root. Prayer reminds us we are not alone to face the challenges, solve the problems, and complete the tasks. We have help from Almighty God!

Take a moment each day to pray and reflect. In this purposeful focus of attention toward God's involvement with you, new horizons will appear. Jesus brings good things to our lives. He desires the best for us. As your prayers grow, your awareness of Jesus' purpose for you will increase as well.

CHAPTER 1

A NEW BEGINNING

Heavenly Father, open my eyes to see and my heart to understand Your ways. I desire Your truth in my life. Forgive me for my rebellious attitude and stubborn pride. I turn to You today in humble repentance. May my thoughts and dreams be pleasing to You. Guide my steps so that Your best may fill my life and Jesus' name will be exalted through my days on this earth. I rejoice in the majesty of my God. Amen.

1 JOHN 1:9

If we confess our sins, he is faithful and just and will forgive us our sins and purify us from all unrighteousness.

TODAY'S THOUGHTS ABOUT
NEW BEGINNINGS

No matter how badly we have failed,
we can always get up and begin again.
Our God is the God of new beginnings.

Warren Wiersbe

God specializes in giving people a fresh start.

Rick Warren

Endings always bring with them
the possibility of a new beginning.

Allen Jackson

Are you in earnest? Seize this very minute.
What you can do, or dream you can, begin it.
Boldness has genius, power, and magic in it.

Goethe

Begin where we will, God is there first.

A. W. Tozer

It is not necessary to be in a big place
to do big things.

Billy Sunday

One of God's glorious gifts to mankind is to
bestow upon him the dawn of a new year.
New opportunities and challenges are before him,
along with a chance to try again.

Mrs. Charles E. Cowman

God is not running an antique shop!
He is making all things new!

Vance Havner

What saves a man is to take a step.
Then another step.

C. S. Lewis

Date:_____

Let's Give Thanks: Today I am thankful for . . .

_____

_____

_____

_____

_____

Let's Trust God: Today I will lay aside my worries and anxieties regarding . . .

_____

_____

_____

_____

Let's Pray: Today I will pray for . . .

_____

_____

_____

_____

_____

_____

CHAPTER 2

JESUS IS LORD

Heavenly Father, I am a sinner and I need a Savior. I believe Jesus is Your son. I believe He died on a cross for my sin. I believe You raised Him to life for my justification. Jesus, be Lord of my life and forgive my sin. I forgive any who have sinned against me. I choose to yield to the lordship of Jesus of Nazareth, to serve Him with all that I am. Amen.

ROMANS 10:9–10

That if you confess with your mouth, "Jesus is Lord," and believe in your heart that God raised him from the dead, you will be saved. For it is with your heart that you believe and are justified, and it is with your mouth that you confess and are saved.

TODAY'S THOUGHTS ABOUT OUR LORD

The central message of the Bible is Jesus Christ.

Billy Graham

Christ is either Lord of all,
or He is not Lord at all.

Hudson Taylor

Any opportunity you have to honor the Lord
with your life will bring greater benefits
to you in time and eternity than
anything else you can do for yourself.

Allen Jackson

Tell me the story of Jesus.
Write on my heart every word.
Tell me the story most precious,
sweetest that ever was heard.

Fanny Crosby

Jesus gives us hope because He keeps us company,
has a vision and knows the way we should go.

Max Lucado

The crucial question for each of us is this:
What do you think of Jesus, and do you yet have
a personal acquaintance with Him?

Hannah Whitall Smith

I am truly happy with Jesus Christ.
I couldn't live without Him.
When my life gets beyond the ability to cope,
He takes over.

Ruth Bell Graham

Christ has turned all our sunsets into dawns.

Clement of Alexandria

Jesus Christ is the first and last, author and finisher,
beginning and end, alpha and omega, and by Him
all other things hold together. He must be first or
nothing. God never comes next!

Vance Havner

Date:_____

Let's Give Thanks: Today I am thankful for . . .

_____

_____

_____

_____

_____

Let's Trust God: Today I will lay aside my worries and anxieties regarding . . .

_____

_____

_____

_____

Let's Pray: Today I will pray for . . .

_____

_____

_____

_____

_____

_____

CHAPTER 3

ANOINTING

Almighty God, send Your anointing upon my life. May the words of my mouth, the thoughts of my heart, and the activity of my life be pleasing in Your sight. Open my eyes to see with Your perspective. Grant me a willing spirit that I would not rebel against Your invitations. Holy Spirit, direct my path toward wisdom and life. I choose to live for the glory of God, to give praise to the Creator of all things, and to rejoice in the majesty of the Holy God. Let everything that has breath praise the Lord!

2 CORINTHIANS 1:22–23

Now it is God who makes both us and you stand firm in Christ. He anointed us, set his seal of ownership on us, and put his Spirit in our hearts as a deposit, guaranteeing what is to come.

TODAY'S THOUGHTS ABOUT GOD'S ANOINTING

If we seek salvation, we are taught by
the very name of Jesus that it is "of him."
If we seek any other gifts of the Spirit,
they will be found in his anointing.

John Calvin

Without the anointing of the Holy Spirit,
the preacher may storm, the teacher may strive,
the Christian worker may sweat,
but all to no avail.

Vance Havner

The power of God through His Spirit will work
within us to the degree that we permit it.

Mrs. Charles E. Cowman

God is looking for imperfect men and women
who have learned to walk in moment-by-moment
dependence on the Holy Spirit.

Charles Stanley

The Holy Spirit is like a living and
continually flowing fountain in believers.
We have the boundless privilege of tapping into
that fountain every time we pray.

Shirley Dobson

God calls us to do his work, proclaiming
his Word to people he loves under the anointing
power of the Holy Spirit to produce results
that only he can bring about.

Jim Cymbala

Love not the world, nor the things that are in
the world. You have an anointing from
the Holy One: live by it! Give yourself to God;
live for him wholly and utterly.

Watchman Nee

The Holy Ghost does not flow through methods,
but through men. He does not come on machinery,
but on men. He does not anoint plans,
but men, men of prayer.

E. M. Bounds

Date:_____

Let's Give Thanks: Today I am thankful for . . .

_____

_____

_____

_____

_____

Let's Trust God: Today I will lay aside my worries and anxieties regarding . . .

_____

_____

_____

_____

Let's Pray: Today I will pray for . . .

_____

_____

_____

_____

_____

_____

CHAPTER 4

LIVING SACRIFICE

Heavenly Father, thank You for calling me into Your Kingdom. I rejoice in my salvation. Your grace and mercy have brought deliverance to my life. You have lifted me from despair and given me hope. Today, I offer myself as a living sacrifice. May my days under the sun bring glory and honor to the name of Jesus. Give me courage to persevere, the wisdom to follow, and the boldness to speak. May Your Kingdom come and Your will be done. Amen.

ROMANS 12:1–2

Therefore, I urge you, brothers, in view of God's mercy, to offer your bodies as living sacrifices, holy and pleasing to God—this is your spiritual act of worship. Do not conform any longer to the pattern of this world, but be transformed by the renewing of your mind. Then you will be able to test and approve what God's will is—his good, pleasing and perfect will.

TODAY'S THOUGHTS ABOUT SERVING GOD WITH AN OBEDIENT HEART

So many times we say that we can't serve God
because we aren't whatever is needed.
We're not talented enough or smart enough or
whatever. But if you are in covenant with
Jesus Christ, He is responsible for covering
your weaknesses, for being your strength.

Kay Arthur

A non-serving Christian is
a contradiction in terms.

Rick Warren

Show me your hands.
Do they have scars from giving?
Show me your feet.
Are they wounded in service?
Show me your heart.
Have you left a place for divine love?

Fulton J. Sheen

True faith commits us to obedience.

A. W. Tozer

Jesus is Victor. Calvary is the place of victory.
Obedience is the pathway of victory. Bible study
and prayer is the preparation for victory.

Corrie ten Boom

In Jesus the service of God and the service of
the least of the brethren were one.

Dietrich Bonhoeffer

Mary could not have dreamed all that would
result from her faithful obedience.
Likewise, you cannot possibly imagine all that
God has in store for you when you trust him.

Henry Blackaby

Have thy tools ready; God will find thee work.

Charles Kingsley

Date:_____

Let's Give Thanks: Today I am thankful for . . .

_____

_____

_____

_____

_____

Let's Trust God: Today I will lay aside my worries and anxieties regarding . . .

_____

_____

_____

_____

Let's Pray: Today I will pray for . . .

_____

_____

_____

_____

_____

_____

CHAPTER 5

FORGIVENESS

Lord, I forgive (name of person) for (name the specifics). I take authority over the enemy, and in the name of Jesus Christ and by the power of His Holy Spirit, I take back the ground I have allowed Satan to gain in my life because of my attitude toward (the person) and give this ground back to my Lord Jesus Christ. I thank You that I am forgiven, and I choose to forgive all others. In Jesus' name, amen.

MATTHEW 6:14–15

For if you forgive men when they sin against you, your heavenly Father will also forgive you. But if you do not forgive men their sins, your Father will not forgive your sins.

TODAY'S THOUGHTS ABOUT FORGIVENESS

Forgiveness is an act of the will,
and the will can function regardless
of the temperature of the heart.

Corrie ten Boom

Forgiveness is man's deepest need
and highest achievement.

Horace Bushnell

Don't let a bitter root grown in your heart or
it will shield you from the generosity of God.

Allen Jackson

Forgiveness is one of the most beautiful words
in the human vocabulary.
How much pain could be avoided
if we all learned the meaning of this word!

Billy Graham

Give me such love for God and men
as will blot out all hatred and bitterness.

Dietrich Bonhoeffer

There is no torment like the inner torment
of an unforgiving spirit. It refuses to be soothed;
it refuses to be healed; it refuses to forget.

Charles Swindoll

Never succumb to the temptation
of bitterness.

Martin Luther King Jr.

When you forgive, you must cancel the debt.
Do not spend your life paying
and collecting debts.

Joyce Meyer

Forgiveness is God's command.

Martin Luther

Date:_____

Let's Give Thanks: Today I am thankful for . . .

_____

_____

_____

_____

_____

Let's Trust God: Today I will lay aside my worries and anxieties regarding . . .

_____

_____

_____

_____

Let's Pray: Today I will pray for . . .

_____

_____

_____

_____

_____

_____

CHAPTER 6

UNBELIEF

Heavenly Father, help my unbelief. May the Word of God come alive within me as never before. As we pray and seek Your face, confirm Your word in our midst. May the power of God be made evident—convict, heal, restore, and deliver. Our hope is in You, our God and our Redeemer. May the name of Jesus be glorified in our generation. It is in His name we pray. Amen.

MARK 9:23–24

"If you can?" said Jesus. "Everything is possible for him who believes." Immediately the boy's father exclaimed, "I do believe; help me overcome my unbelief!"

TODAY'S THOUGHTS ABOUT UNBELIEF

What I believe about God
is the most important thing about me.

A. W. Tozer

Ignoring Him by neglecting prayer
and Bible reading will cause you to doubt.

Anne Graham Lotz

What you believe about Jesus matters.

Allen Jackson

Have a sincere desire to serve God
and mankind, and stop doubting.
Stop thinking negatively.
Simply start living by faith,
pray earnestly and humbly,
and get into the habit
of looking expectantly for the best.

Norman Vincent Peale

You never know how much you really believe
anything until its truth or falsehood becomes
a matter of life and death to you.

C. S. Lewis

Faith is born at the Cross of Christ.

C. H. Spurgeon

The people who really rule the world
are those who know how to pray.

Derek Prince

The Bible teaches that when we turn our backs
on God and choose to disregard His moral laws
there are inevitable consequences.

Billy Graham

Unconfessed sin in your life
will cause you to doubt.

Anne Graham Lotz

Date: _____

Let's Give Thanks: Today I am thankful for . . .

_____

_____

_____

_____

_____

Let's Trust God: Today I will lay aside my worries and anxieties regarding . . .

_____

_____

_____

_____

Let's Pray: Today I will pray for . . .

_____

_____

_____

_____

_____

_____

CHAPTER 7

PROTECTION

I rejoice in God my protector. Almighty God is my shield and my strength. His grace and mercy sustain me. The Holy Spirit is my helper. Through the blood of Jesus, I have been delivered out of the hand of the enemy. My life is secure in the hands of my Creator. My hope is anchored in the faithfulness of my Lord and Redeemer, Jesus Christ. Amen.

PSALM 91:1–2

He who dwells in the shelter of the Most High will rest in the shadow of the Almighty. I will say of the LORD, "He is my refuge and my fortress, my God, in whom I trust."

TODAY'S THOUGHTS ABOUT GOD'S PROTECTION

Discipline yourself to stay close to God.
He alone is your security.

Billy Graham

The center of God's will is our only safety.

Corrie ten Boom

No difficulties can baffle Him if you will only
put yourselves absolutely into His hands
and let Him have His own way with you.

Hannah Whitall Smith

Seeing that a pilot steers the ship in which we sail,
who will never allow us to perish even in
the midst of shipwrecks, there is no reason why
our minds should be overwhelmed with fear
and overcome with weariness.

John Calvin

Where does your security lie? Is God your refuge,
your hiding place, your stronghold, your shepherd,
your counselor, your friend, your redeemer,
your savior, your guide?
If He is, you don't need to search
any further for security.

Elisabeth Elliot

A mighty fortress is our God,
a bulwark never failing; our helper he amid
the flood of mortal ills prevailing.

Martin Luther

A God wise enough to create me and the world
I live in is wise enough to watch out for me.

Phillip Yancey

Seek your security in anything
but God and you will never find it.

St. Stephen of Muret

Date:_____

Let's Give Thanks: Today I am thankful for . . .

_____

_____

_____

_____

_____

Let's Trust God: Today I will lay aside my worries and anxieties regarding . . .

_____

_____

_____

_____

Let's Pray: Today I will pray for . . .

_____

_____

_____

_____

_____

_____

CHAPTER 8

HEALING

Heavenly Father, let faith arise in my heart. Grant me a willing spirit to cooperate with You. May Your promises become my reality. I put my trust in You. I turn away from anything that separates me from your best. I believe You bring life and health to my entire being. I rest in Your abundant provision for my life. May a spirit of generosity grow within me. I choose to live for the glory of the Almighty God. In Jesus' name, amen.

3 JOHN 1:2

Dear friend, I pray that you may enjoy good health and that all may go well with you, even as your soul is getting along well.

TODAY'S THOUGHTS ABOUT HEALING AND HEALTH

God wants you to give Him your body.
Some people do foolish things with their bodies.
God wants your body as a holy sacrifice.

Warren Wiersbe

Eat to live and not live to eat.

Ben Franklin

A Christian should no more defile his body
than a Jew would defile the temple.

Warren Wiersbe

Think health; eat sparingly;
exercise regularly; walk a lot;
and, think positively about yourself.

Norman Vincent Peale

Let's Pray

Stay busy. Get proper exercise.
Eat the right foods.
Don't spend time watching TV,
lying in bed, or napping all day.

Truett Cathy

God can heal a body; God can change a life;
God can restore a family. God is able.

Allen Jackson

It is wonderful what miracles God works in wills
that are utterly surrendered to Him.

Hannah Whitall Smith

Ultimate healing and the glorification
of the body are certainly among the blessings
of Calvary for the believing Christian.
Immediate healing is not guaranteed.

Warren Wiersbe

Date:_____

Let's Give Thanks: Today I am thankful for . . .

_____

_____

_____

_____

_____

Let's Trust God: Today I will lay aside my worries and anxieties regarding . . .

_____

_____

_____

_____

Let's Pray: Today I will pray for . . .

_____

_____

_____

_____

_____

_____

CHAPTER 9

LIVING ABUNDANTLY

Heavenly Father, thank You for Your generous provision for my life. You have given generously that I may live abundantly. Forgive me for selfish ambition and greed. Today I offer myself as a living sacrifice. May the invitations of God be more real to me than the invitations of this world. I choose to live for the glory of my King. I lay down all anxiety and stress. My future is secure and my provision complete because I rest in the hands of the Creator of all things. In Jesus' name, amen.

2 CORINTHIANS 9:6–8

Remember this: Whoever sows sparingly will also reap sparingly, and whoever sows generously will also reap generously. Each man should give what he has decided in his heart to give, not reluctantly or under compulsion, for God loves a cheerful giver. And God is able to make all grace abound to you, so that in all things at all times, having all that you need, you will abound in every good work.

TODAY'S THOUGHTS ABOUT GOD'S ABUNDANCE

Those who have been truly converted to
Jesus Christ know the meaning of abundant living.

Billy Graham

Instead of living a black-and-white existence,
we'll be released into a Technicolor world of
vibrancy and emotion when we more accurately
reflect His nature to the world around us.

Bill Hybels

Jesus wants Life for us; Life with a capital L.

John Eldredge

The man who lives without Jesus is the poorest
of the poor, whereas no one is so rich
as the man who lives in His grace.

Thomas à Kempis

God loves you and wants you to experience
peace and life—abundant and eternal.

Billy Graham

You can choose whether you want to make
your way or you're going to trust
God's abundant provision.

Allen Jackson

We honor God by asking for great things
when they are a part of His promise.
We dishonor Him and cheat ourselves
when we ask for molehills
where He has promised mountains.

Vance Havner

God is the giver, and we are the receivers.
And His richest gifts are bestowed not upon those
who do the greatest things, but upon those who
accept His abundance and His grace.

Hannah Whitall Smith

Date:_____

Let's Give Thanks: Today I am thankful for . . .

_____

_____

_____

_____

_____

Let's Trust God: Today I will lay aside my worries and anxieties regarding . . .

_____

_____

_____

_____

Let's Pray: Today I will pray for . . .

_____

_____

_____

_____

_____

_____

CHAPTER 10

OUR NATION

Heavenly Father, forgive us for ignoring Your counsel and choosing our own way. We have turned our backs on Your goodness and abundant blessings. We have chosen pride and indulgence over righteousness and purity. We humble ourselves today in repentance, asking for mercy. We are a nation in need of healing. Only Almighty God can restore our fortunes. We do not blame others for our circumstances; we have walked this path. This day we acknowledge Almighty God as the judge of all the earth. May the name of Jesus of Nazareth be lifted up in our homes, our city, our state, and our nation. In Jesus' name, amen.

1 TIMOTHY 2:1–5; 8

I urge, then, first of all, that requests, prayers, intercession and thanksgiving be made for everyone—for kings and all those in authority, that we may live peaceful and quiet lives in all godliness and holiness. This is good, and pleases God our Savior, who wants all men to be saved and to come to a knowledge of the truth. For there is one God and one mediator between God and men, the man Christ Jesus . . . I want men everywhere to lift up holy hands in prayer, without anger or disputing.

TODAY'S THOUGHTS ABOUT THE POWER OF PRAYER

Prayer is the hard-work business of Christianity, and it nets amazing results.

David Jeremiah

The strength of our nation comes from a history of faith in God.

Allen Jackson

God's solution is just a prayer away!

Max Lucado

If the spiritual life be healthy,
under the full power of the Holy Spirit,
praying without ceasing will be natural.

Andrew Murray

Two wings are necessary to lift our souls
toward God: prayer and praise.
Prayer asks. Praise accepts the answer.

Mrs. Charles E. Cowman

It is impossible to overstate the need
for prayer in the fabric of family life.

James Dobson

Don't pray when you feel like it.
Have an appointment with the Lord and keep it.

Corrie ten Boom

If you lack knowledge, go to school.
If you lack wisdom, get on your knees!

Vance Havner

Date:_____

Let's Give Thanks: Today I am thankful for . . .

_____

_____

_____

_____

_____

Let's Trust God: Today I will lay aside my worries
and anxieties regarding . . .

_____

_____

_____

_____

Let's Pray: Today I will pray for . . .

_____

_____

_____

_____

_____

_____

CHAPTER 11

ASKING FOR GOD'S WISDOM

Heavenly Father, thank you for the many ways You have intervened on my behalf. In Your great mercy You have provided hope and purpose to my journey. Give me wisdom to lead an overcoming life. May Your power be made evident in all I do. Give me eyes to see and ears to listen. I rejoice in my Lord and my Redeemer. In Jesus' name, amen.

JAMES 1:5

If any of you lacks wisdom, he should ask God, who gives generously to all without finding fault, and it will be given to him.

TODAY'S THOUGHTS ABOUT GOD'S WISDOM

Knowledge is horizontal. Wisdom is vertical;
it comes down from above.

Billy Graham

Wisdom is the right use of knowledge.
To know is not to be wise.
There is no fool so great as the knowing fool.
But, to know how to use knowledge
is to have wisdom.

C. H. Spurgeon

Wise people listen to wise instruction, especially
instruction from the Word of God.

Warren Wiersbe

Knowledge is not wisdom.
Wisdom is the proper use of knowledge.

Vance Havner

If we neglect the Bible, we cannot expect
to benefit from the wisdom and direction
that result from knowing God's Word.

Vonette Bright

You see, between us and God's wisdom is a valley,
a place of humility. We have to lay aside
worldly wisdom. We have to become fools
in the eyes of the world in order that we
may really enter into God's wisdom.

Derek Prince

The entire sum of our wisdom, of that which
deserves to be called true and certain wisdom,
may be said to consist of two parts:
the knowledge of God and of ourselves.

John Calvin

When we speak about wisdom,
we are speaking about Christ.

St. Ambrose

Date:_____

Let's Give Thanks: Today I am thankful for . . .

_____

_____

_____

_____

_____

Let's Trust God: Today I will lay aside my worries and anxieties regarding . . .

_____

_____

_____

_____

Let's Pray: Today I will pray for . . .

_____

_____

_____

_____

_____

CHAPTER 12

LIFE DIRECTION

Heavenly Father, Your wisdom and strength are a great comfort to me. I know nothing is too hard for You. You strengthen the weak, comfort the weary, and deliver the oppressed. Holy Spirit, open my heart to the invitations of God. Help me to recognize His pathway. I choose to yield to God's purposes for life. Lead me in paths of righteousness that are pleasing to You. May my life bring honor and glory to my Lord. In Jesus' name, amen.

PSALM 86:11

Teach me your way, O LORD, and I will walk in your truth; give me an undivided heart, that I may fear your name.

TODAY'S THOUGHTS ABOUT GOD'S GUIDANCE

We have ample evidence that the Lord is able
to guide. The promises cover every imaginable
situation. All we need to do is to take
the hand he stretches out.

Elisabeth Elliot

The will of God will never take us where
the grace of God cannot sustain us.

Billy Graham

We should not be upset when unexpected
and upsetting things happen.
God, in His wisdom, means to make
something of us which we have not yet attained
and is dealing with us accordingly.

J. I. Packer

God is the silent partner in all great enterprises.

Abraham Lincoln

Time spent in prayer will yield more than that
given to work. Prayer alone gives work its worth
and its success. Prayer opens the way for God
Himself to do His work in us and through us.

Andrew Murray

You will not fulfill your life assignment as
a Christ-follower until you make
the commitment to be a person of prayer
and to honor the Word of God.

Allen Jackson

Some of us can only hear God in the thunder
of revivals or in public worship;
we have to learn to listen to God's voice in
the ordinary circumstances of life.

Oswald Chambers

When we are obedient,
God guides our steps and our stops.

Corrie ten Boom

Date:_____

Let's Give Thanks: Today I am thankful for . . .

_____

_____

_____

_____

_____

Let's Trust God: Today I will lay aside my worries and anxieties regarding . . .

_____

_____

_____

_____

Let's Pray: Today I will pray for . . .

_____

_____

_____

_____

_____

_____

CHAPTER 13

DELIVERANCE

Today I lay aside the spirit of heaviness and raise my voice in praise of the Lord—my strength and my Redeemer. May my eyes be opened to the provision of God and my ears attentive to the sound of His deliverance. Holy Spirit, help me. In You I find power and revelation. Let the people of God arise triumphant, and may the name of Jesus be lifted up throughout the earth. In Jesus' name, amen.

ROMANS 8:1–2

Therefore, there is now no condemnation for those who are in Christ Jesus, because through Christ Jesus the law of the Spirit of life set me free from the law of sin and death.

TODAY'S THOUGHTS ABOUT GOD'S DELIVERANCE

No situation is beyond God's control.
Over my wife's desk are these words:
"Fear not for the future. God is already there."

Billy Graham

As sure as ever God puts His children in
the furnace, He will be in the furnace with them.

C. H. Spurgeon

Don't let obstacles along the road to eternity
shake your confidence in God's promises.

David Jeremiah

God is trying to get a message through to you,
and the message is: "Stop depending on inadequate
human resources. Let me handle the matter."

Catherine Marshall

Let's Pray

As you walk through the valley of the unknown,
you will find the footprints of Jesus
both in front of you and beside you.

Charles Stanley

I refuse to become panicky, as I lift up my eyes
to Him and accept it as coming from
the throne of God for some great purpose
of blessing to my own heart.

Alan Redpath

No difficulties can baffle Him if you will only
put yourselves absolutely into His hands
and let Him have His own way with you.

Hannah Whitall Smith

Faith is not merely holding on to God.
It is God holding on to you.

Corrie ten Boom

Date:_____

Let's Give Thanks: Today I am thankful for . . .

_____

_____

_____

_____

_____

Let's Trust God: Today I will lay aside my worries and anxieties regarding . . .

_____

_____

_____

_____

Let's Pray: Today I will pray for . . .

_____

_____

_____

_____

_____

_____

CHAPTER 14

STRENGTHEN THE CHURCH

Heavenly Father, surely Your plans and purposes will be made known in all the earth. Strengthen Your servants in this generation. Respond to those who cry out to You, deliver the oppressed, and refresh the weary. Establish Your Word with power and authority. Let a harvest of righteousness begin. Raise up leaders to cooperate with Your Spirit. May the Church reflect the glory of our Lord and King as never before. In Jesus name, amen.

MATTHEW 16:19

"I will give you the keys of the kingdom of heaven; whatever you bind on earth will be bound in heaven, and whatever you loose on earth will be loosed in heaven."

TODAY'S THOUGHTS ABOUT THE CHURCH

The Bible knows nothing of solitary religion.

John Wesley

The value of the Church of Jesus Christ
in the earth is to be a peculiar people—a people
who recognize the sovereignty of God,
the majesty of God—who live under
an awareness of the fear of the Lord.

Allen Jackson

Every believer is commanded to be
plugged in to a local church.

David Jeremiah

The church's job is to equip the saints
for works of service in the world.

Charles Colson

And how can we improve the church?
Simply and only by improving ourselves.

A. W. Tozer

What the church needs is not better machinery
nor new organizations, but instead it needs men
whom the Holy Spirit can use—
men of prayer, men mighty in prayer.

E. M. Bounds

Only participation in the full life
of a local church builds spiritual muscle.

Rick Warren

It has always been the work of the church
to bring others to belief in Christ and to experience
a personal relationship with Him.

Charles Stanley

The church is where it's at.
The first place of Christian service for
any Christian is in a local church.

Jerry Clower

Nothing will bring freedom and liberty to the life
of a human being in a more profound way than
a true expression of the Church of Jesus Christ.

Allen Jackson

Date:_____

Let's Give Thanks: Today I am thankful for . . .

_____

_____

_____

_____

_____

Let's Trust God: Today I will lay aside my worries
and anxieties regarding . . .

_____

_____

_____

_____

Let's Pray: Today I will pray for . . .

_____

_____

_____

_____

_____

_____

CHAPTER 15

CHOOSING CONTENTMENT

Heavenly Father, I choose to yield to You today as one being taught. Holy Spirit, help me. I repent of pride, self-righteousness, and complacency. I will walk in the truth I know. My desire is to be a disciple of Jesus Christ and live a life that is pleasing in God's sight. Through my life, may the name of Jesus be exalted and His kingdom extended. In Jesus' name, amen.

1 TIMOTHY 4:6

But godliness with contentment is great gain.

HEBREWS 13:5

Keep your lives free from the love of money and be content with what you have, because God has said, "Never will I leave you; never will I forsake you."

TODAY'S THOUGHTS ABOUT CONTENTMENT

When you truly know God,
you have energy to serve him,
boldness to share him, and contentment in him.

J. I. Packer

Those who are God's without reserve are,
in every sense, content.

Hannah Whitall Smith

Next to faith this is the highest art:
to be content with the calling
in which God has placed you.

Martin Luther

Happy is the person who has learned the secret
of being content with whatever life brings him.

Billy Graham

The antidote for covetousness is contentment.
The two are in opposition. Whereas the covetous,
greedy person worships himself,
the contented person worships God.
Contentment comes from trusting God.

John MacArthur

Contentment is possible
when we stop striving for more.

Charles Swindoll

Contentment does not come from having much;
we could argue that the more you have the more
discontent you can become.

Allen Jackson

Contentment is something we learn by adhering to
the basics—cultivating a growing relationship
with Jesus Christ, living daily, and knowing that
Christ strengthens us for every challenge.

Charles Stanley

Date: _____

Let's Give Thanks: Today I am thankful for . . .

_____

_____

_____

_____

_____

Let's Trust God: Today I will lay aside my worries and anxieties regarding . . .

_____

_____

_____

_____

Let's Pray: Today I will pray for . . .

_____

_____

_____

_____

_____

_____

CHAPTER 16

HUNGER FOR YOUR WORD

Heavenly Father, may Your Word come alive within me. May my heart be open to Your instruction. Give me a willing spirit to cooperate with You. I choose to honor You in all my ways. Holy Spirit, open my eyes to see and my heart to understand the great privilege of serving the living God. In Jesus' name, amen.

PROVERBS 2:1–5

My son, if you accept my words and store up my commands within you, turning your ear to wisdom and applying your heart to understanding, and if you call out for insight and cry aloud for understanding, and if you look for it as for silver and search for it as for hidden treasure, then you will understand the fear of the LORD and find the knowledge of God.

TODAY'S THOUGHTS ABOUT GOD'S WORD

Make it the first morning business of your life
to understand some part of the Bible clearly,
and make it your daily business to obey it.

John Ruskin

Prayer and the Word are inseparably
linked together. Power in the use of either
depends on the presence of the other.

Andrew Murray

Invest time in the Word of God;
it will illuminate your life and your life plans.

Allen Jackson

God's Book is packed with overwhelming riches.
They are unsearchable—the more we have,
the more there is to have.

Oswald Chambers

Nobody ever outgrows the scriptures;
the book widens and deepens with our years.

C. H. Spurgeon

The Bible grows more beautiful
as we grow in our understanding of it.

Goethe

Israel is a testimony to the faithfulness
of God and His Word.

Allen Jackson

Make the Bible part of your daily life,
and ask God to engrave its truths on your soul.

Billy Graham

The Scriptures were not given for our information,
but for our transformation.

D. L. Moody

Date:_____

Let's Give Thanks: Today I am thankful for . . .

_____

_____

_____

_____

_____

Let's Trust God: Today I will lay aside my worries and anxieties regarding . . .

_____

_____

_____

_____

Let's Pray: Today I will pray for . . .

_____

_____

_____

_____

_____

_____

CHAPTER 17

BE A DISCIPLE

My choice is to be a disciple of Jesus Christ, to live for His honor. Father, I pray that I may know the truth. I choose Your freedom in my life, for my family and in my home. Lord, guide me in Your truth. May my entire family be led by Your truth. May I continually walk in Your truth—in my marriage, in my business, in all of my relationships, throughout my entire life. Father, wherever I may have strayed from Your truth, teach me. My desire is to walk before You in truth. Wherever my heart is divided, teach me to fear Your name. I thank You that You hear my prayers, that You are attentive to my life, and that I am not alone. I choose to invest my life, my resources, and my energy—all that I am, in the pursuit of Your truth. Amen.

PROVERBS 23:23

Buy the truth and do not sell it; get wisdom, discipline and understanding.

TODAY'S THOUGHTS ABOUT DISCIPLESHIP

A disciple is a follower of Christ.
That means you take on His priorities as your own.
His agenda becomes your agenda.
His mission becomes your mission.

Charles Stanley

Jesus challenges you and me to keep
our focus daily on the cross of His will
if we want to be His disciples.

Anne Graham Lotz

To be a disciple of Jesus means to learn from Him,
to follow Him. The cost may be high.

Billy Graham

His voice leads us not into timid discipleship
but into bold witness.

Charles Stanley

Let's Pray

As we seek to become disciples of Jesus Christ,
we should never forget that the word *disciple*
is directly related to the word discipline.
To be a disciple of the Lord Jesus Christ
is to know his discipline.

Dennis Swanberg

Our Lord's conception of discipleship
is not that we work for God,
but that God works through us.

Oswald Chambers

Discipleship is a decision to live by
what I know about God, not by what I feel
about him or myself or my neighbors.

Eugene Peterson

The Bible says that being a Christian
is not only a great way to die,
but it's also the best way to live.

Bill Hybels

Date:_____

Let's Give Thanks: Today I am thankful for . . .

_____

_____

_____

_____

_____

Let's Trust God: Today I will lay aside my worries and anxieties regarding . . .

_____

_____

_____

_____

Let's Pray: Today I will pray for . . .

_____

_____

_____

_____

_____

_____

CHAPTER 18

CHOOSE THE TRUTH

Father, bring wisdom, discipline, and understanding to my life. Father, I choose to be led by Your Spirit of Truth. Help me to recognize His leading, to discern His voice, to understand His direction. My desire is to honor the Spirit of Truth in my life. I pray that I would in no way suppress the truth. In my home and life may Your truth have free reign. In Jesus' name may godlessness and wickedness be cast out and truth be triumphant. May Your truth find full expression in my life, my home, and my family. Direct my steps that I may obey Your truth and grow up into all you created me for. I choose to stand firmly with the belt of truth in place in my life. Thank You for Your truth and the freedom it is bringing into my life.

JOHN 8:32

"Then you will know the truth, and the truth will set you free."

TODAY'S THOUGHTS ABOUT TRUTH

Where I found truth, there found I my God,
who is the truth itself.

St. Augustine

The best way to be protected
against deception is to know the Truth.

Allen Jackson

The Kingdom of God runs on truth,
not sentiment.

Edwin Louis Cole

Let us rejoice in the truth,
wherever we find its lamp burning.

Albert Schweitzer

Peace if possible, but truth at any rate.

Martin Luther

Rationalization: It's what we do when we
substitute false explanations for true reasons.
It's when we cloud our actual motives
with nice-sounding excuses.

Charles Swindoll

The greatest friend of truth is time,
her greatest enemy is prejudice,
and her constant companion humility.

Charles Colson

Learning God's truth and getting it
into our heads is one thing,
but living God's truth and getting it
into our characters is quite something else.

Warren Wiersbe

Truth will triumph.
The Father of truth will win,
and the followers of truth will be saved.

Max Lucado

Date:_____

Let's Give Thanks: Today I am thankful for . . .

_____

_____

_____

_____

_____

Let's Trust God: Today I will lay aside my worries and anxieties regarding . . .

_____

_____

_____

_____

Let's Pray: Today I will pray for . . .

_____

_____

_____

_____

_____

_____

CHAPTER 19

BLOOD OF JESUS DECLARATION

I agree with what the Word of God says the blood does for me:

- Through the blood of Jesus, all my sins are forgiven.
- Through the blood of Jesus, I am redeemed out of the hand of the Devil.
- Through the blood of Jesus, I am continually being cleansed from all sins.
- Through the blood of Jesus, I am justified, made righteous, just as if I'd never sinned.
- Through the blood of Jesus, I am sanctified, made holy, set apart to God.
- My body is a temple of Your Holy Spirit— redeemed, cleansed, and sanctified by the blood of Jesus.
- The devil has no place in me, no power over me, and no unsettled claims against me. All has been settled by the blood of Jesus.

Adapted from Derek Prince's
Declaration of Confidence in God's Protection

REVELATION 12:11

They overcame him by the blood of the Lamb and by
the word of their testimony; they did not love their lives
so much as to shrink from death.

TODAY'S THOUGHTS ABOUT
CHRIST'S SACRIFICE

The cross means this: Jesus taking our place
to satisfy the demands of God's justice
and turning aside God's wrath.

James Montgomery Boice

The sacrifice of the Lamb
is absolutely sufficient in itself
to take away our sin and reconcile us to God.

Anne Graham Lotz

Jesus Christ opened heaven's door for us
by His death on the cross.

Billy Graham

Let's Pray

Mount Calvary is the academy of love.

St. Francis de Sales

There was One, who for "us sinners
and our salvation," left the glories of heaven
and sojourned upon this earth in
weariness and woe, amid those
who hated him and finally took his life.

Lottie Moon

Man seeks to win his glory by the sacrifices of
others, Christ by the sacrifice of Himself.

C. H. Spurgeon

He loved us not because we're lovable,
but because He is love.

C. S. Lewis

Live your lives in love, the same sort of love which
Christ gives us, and which He perfectly expressed
when He gave Himself as a sacrifice to God.

Corrie ten Boom

Date:_____

Let's Give Thanks: Today I am thankful for . . .

_____

_____

_____

_____

_____

Let's Trust God: Today I will lay aside my worries and anxieties regarding . . .

_____

_____

_____

_____

Let's Pray: Today I will pray for . . .

_____

_____

_____

_____

_____

_____

CHAPTER 20

GOD'S PROTECTION

I rejoice in the protection of Almighty God over my life. I am the Lord's servant; I rest in the completeness of His strength and care. No weapon formed against me will prevail. I will refute every tongue that rises against me; this is my heritage as a servant of the Lord. A thousand may fall at my side, but destruction will not overwhelm me. I have made the Most High my dwelling place. God is my refuge and my security. No harm will befall me, no disaster will overtake me. God has commanded His angels to watch over my life. My life and my future are secure through the strength of my Lord and my Redeemer.

ISAIAH 54:17

"No weapon forged against you will prevail, and you will refute every tongue that accuses you. This is the heritage of the servants of the LORD, and this is their vindication from me," declares the LORD.

PSALM 91:7–11

A thousand may fall at your side, ten thousand at your right hand, but it will not come near you. You will only observe with your eyes and see the punishment of the wicked. If you make the Most High your dwelling— even the LORD, who is my refuge—then no harm will befall you, no disaster will come near your tent. For he will command his angels concerning you to guard you in all your ways.

TODAY'S THOUGHTS ABOUT GOD'S PROTECTION

The Lord God of heaven and earth, the Almighty Creator of all things, He who holds the universe in His hand as though it were a very little thing, He is your Shepherd, and He has charged Himself with the care and keeping of you.

Hannah Whitall Smith

The Rock of Ages is the great sheltering encirclement.

Oswald Chambers

God's provision for His people is complete.
He sent His son to a brutal death because
you and I needed tremendous help.

Allen Jackson

God delights in spreading His protective wings
and enfolding His frightened, weary,
beaten-down, worn-out children.

Bill Hybels

There is not only fear, but terrible danger,
for the life unguarded by God.

Oswald Chambers

God is always sufficient in
perfect proportion to our need.

Beth Moore

There are four words I wish we would never forget,
and they are, "God keeps his word."

Charles Swindoll

Date:

Let's Give Thanks: Today I am thankful for . . .

_____

_____

_____

_____

_____

Let's Trust God: Today I will lay aside my worries and anxieties regarding . . .

_____

_____

_____

_____

Let's Pray: Today I will pray for . . .

_____

_____

_____

_____

_____

_____

ACCEPTED BY GOD

I choose Jesus of Nazareth as Lord of my life. Through Jesus I am redeemed out of an empty way of life. I have been delivered from the kingdom of darkness and welcomed into the Kingdom of the living God. God chose me before the creation of the world to be holy and blameless before Him. He has chosen me as a part of His family. God has accepted me as His child. I have been delivered from all rejection. The pain of rejection has no place in me through the power of Jesus' name. I have been redeemed, forgiven, and accepted into the family of Almighty God. I have an inheritance in heaven that can never spoil or be diminished. I rest in God's mercy, love, and provision for me.

COLOSSIANS 1:11–14

Giving thanks to the Father, who has qualified you to share in the inheritance of the saints in the kingdom of light. For he has rescued us from the dominion of darkness and brought us into the kingdom of the Son he loves, in whom we have redemption, the forgiveness of sins.

EPHESIANS 1:3–7

Praise be to the God and Father of our Lord Jesus Christ, who has blessed us in the heavenly realms with every spiritual blessing in Christ. For he chose us in him before the creation of the world to be holy and blameless in his sight. In love he predestined us to be adopted as his sons through Jesus Christ, in accordance with his pleasure and will—to the praise of his glorious grace, which he has freely given us in the One he loves. In him we have redemption through his blood, the forgiveness of sins, in accordance with the riches of God's grace.

TODAY'S THOUGHTS ABOUT GOD'S MERCY AND LOVE

The grace of God is sufficient for all our needs,
for every problem, and for every difficulty, for every
broken heart, and for every human sorrow.

Peter Marshall

God's mercy is boundless, free, and,
through Jesus Christ our Lord,
available to us in our present situation.

A. W. Tozer

It doesn't matter how big the sin is or how small,
it doesn't matter whether it was spontaneous
or malicious. God will forgive you
if you come to Him and confess your sin!

Anne Graham Lotz

The Bible has a simple story.
God made man. Man rejected God.
God won't give up until he wins him back.

Max Lucado

Date:_____

Let's Give Thanks: Today I am thankful for . . .

_____

_____

_____

_____

_____

Let's Trust God: Today I will lay aside my worries and anxieties regarding . . .

_____

_____

_____

_____

Let's Pray: Today I will pray for . . .

_____

_____

_____

_____

_____

_____

CHAPTER 22

HOPE AND ENCOURAGEMENT

I put on the garment of praise and hope. I choose the joy of the Lord as my strength. I lay aside the spirit of heaviness and raise my voice in praise of the living God. May my eyes be opened to the provision of God and my ears attentive to the sound of His deliverance. Holy Spirit, help me. In You I find power and revelation. God has restored my broken heart and set my feet on a path of victory. I have hope for today and the strength to complete the course You have chosen for me. Let the people of God arise triumphant, and may the name of Jesus be lifted up throughout the earth. In Jesus' name, amen.

ISAIAH 61:1–3

He has sent me to bind up the brokenhearted, to proclaim freedom for the captives and release from darkness for the prisoners, to proclaim the year of the Lord's favor and the day of vengeance of our God, to comfort all who mourn, and provide for those who grieve in Zion—to bestow on them a crown of beauty instead of ashes, the oil of gladness instead of mourning, and a garment of praise instead of a spirit of despair. They will be called oaks of righteousness, a planting of the LORD for the display of his splendor.

PSALM 34:18–19

The LORD is close to the brokenhearted and saves those who are crushed in spirit. A righteous man may have many troubles, but the LORD delivers him from them all.

TODAY'S THOUGHTS ABOUT HOPE AND ENCOURAGEMENT

Encouragement is the oxygen of the soul.

John Maxwell

If we can receive the gifts God has for us,
then we can become a conduit for
His gifts to those around us.

Allen Jackson

Hope is nothing more than the expectation
of those things which faith has believed
to be truly promised by God.

John Calvin

Hope looks for the good in people, opens doors
for people, discovers what can be done to help,
lights a candle, does not yield to cynicism.
Hope sets people free.

Barbara Johnson

People are genuinely motivated by hope
and a part of that hope is the assurance
of future glory with God for those
who are His people.

Warren Wiersbe

A lot of people have gone further
than they thought they could because
someone else thought they could.

Zig Ziglar

Date:_____

Let's Give Thanks: Today I am thankful for . . .

_____

_____

_____

_____

_____

Let's Trust God: Today I will lay aside my worries
and anxieties regarding . . .

_____

_____

_____

_____

Let's Pray: Today I will pray for . . .

_____

_____

_____

_____

_____

_____

CHAPTER 23

OUR LEADERS

Almighty God, You set up leaders and remove them. You watch over the course of nations. We come to ask for mercy for our nation. We have been uniquely blessed. We have experienced abundance, peace, and prosperity but we have turned our backs on You. We have been wrong; forgive us. Awaken Your people in this season. Send Your Spirit among us to stir our hearts. No one can stand before Your anger; be merciful to us because of Your great mercy. May the praises of God once again rise from Your people in this land. In Jesus' name, amen.

2 CHRONICLES 7:13-14

"When I shut up the heavens so that there is no rain, or command locusts to devour the land or send a plague among my people, if my people, who are called by my name, will humble themselves and pray and seek my

face and turn from their wicked ways, then will I hear from heaven and will forgive their sin and will heal their land."

TODAY'S THOUGHTS ABOUT LEADERSHIP

Leadership is the knack of getting somebody
to do something you want done
because he wants to do it.

Dwight D. Eisenhower

The test of a leader is taking
the vision from me to we.

John Maxwell

True leaders are not afraid to
surround themselves with people of ability—
and not afraid to give those people
opportunities for greatness.

Warren Wiersbe

You can never separate a leader's actions
from his character.

John Maxwell

A wise leader chooses a variety of gifted individuals.
He complements his strengths.

Charles Stanley

Leaders must learn how to wait.
Often their followers don't always see
as far as they see or have the faith that they have.

Warren Wiersbe

Integrity and maturity are two character traits
vital to the heart of a leader.

Charles Stanley

I never tell my players anything
I don't absolutely believe myself.

Vince Lombardi

Date:_____

Let's Give Thanks: Today I am thankful for . . .

_____

_____

_____

_____

_____

Let's Trust God: Today I will lay aside my worries and anxieties regarding . . .

_____

_____

_____

_____

Let's Pray: Today I will pray for . . .

_____

_____

_____

_____

_____

_____

CHAPTER 24

YIELDING

Heavenly Father, I choose life today. I choose to serve God Almighty, the maker of heaven and earth. I believe Jesus of Nazareth is Your Son, and I choose Him as Lord of all that I am. I choose God's will for my life. Grant me the wisdom to follow, the humility to yield, and the strength to endure. May the fear of the Lord flourish in my heart. In Jesus' name, amen.

JOSHUA 24:14–15

"Now fear the LORD and serve him with all faithfulness. Throw away the gods your forefathers worshiped beyond the River and in Egypt, and serve the LORD. But if serving the LORD seems undesirable to you, then choose for yourselves this day whom you will serve, whether the gods your forefathers served beyond the River, or the gods of the Amorites, in whose land you are living. But as for me and my household, we will serve the LORD."

TODAY'S THOUGHTS ABOUT YIELDING

Anxiety is the natural result when
our hopes are centered in anything short
of God and His will for us.

Billy Graham

The will of God is either a burden we carry
or a power which carries us.

Corrie ten Boom

To walk out of his will is to walk into nowhere.

C. S. Lewis

God is God. Because He is God,
He is worthy of my trust and obedience.
I will find rest nowhere but in His holy will,
a will that is unspeakably beyond
my largest notions of what He is up to.

Elisabeth Elliot

Absolute submission is not enough;
we should go on to joyful acquiescence
to the will of God.

C. H. Spurgeon

The greatest honor of our lives
is to be servants of the Most High God.

Allen Jackson

The only safe place is in the center of God's will.
It is not only the safest place. It is also the most
rewarding and the most satisfying place to be.

Gigi Graham Tchividjian

Nine-tenths of the difficulties are overcome when
our hearts are ready to do the Lord's will.

George Mueller

Before we can pray, "Lord, Thy Kingdom come,"
we must be willing to pray, "My Kingdom go."

Alan Redpath

Date:_____

Let's Give Thanks: Today I am thankful for . . .

_____

_____

_____

_____

_____

Let's Trust God: Today I will lay aside my worries and anxieties regarding . . .

_____

_____

_____

_____

Let's Pray: Today I will pray for . . .

_____

_____

_____

_____

_____

_____

CHAPTER 25

SECURITY IN GOD

Heavenly Father, I rejoice in Your faithfulness. You have chosen a path for me that leads to righteousness and complete fulfillment. I trust Your provision for my life. You are my security. You watch over my days. My life is a testimony to the power of my God, a declaration of Your great love. Holy Spirit, direct my path to a place of triumph and deliver me from every snare. I will rest in the shadow of Your protection. Let the name of Jesus be lifted high, amen.

PSALM 121:1–7

I lift up my eyes to the hills—where does my help come from? My help comes from the LORD, the Maker of heaven and earth. He will not let your foot slip—he who watches over you will not slumber; indeed, he who watches over Israel will neither slumber nor sleep. The LORD watches over you—the LORD is your shade at your right hand; the sun will not harm you by day, nor the moon by night. The LORD *will keep you from all harm—he will watch over your life; the* LORD *will watch over your coming and going both now and forevermore.*

TODAY'S THOUGHTS ABOUT SECURITY IN GOD

The weaker we feel, the harder we lean.
And the harder we lean,
the stronger we grow spiritually.

J. I. Packer

Strive in prayer; let faith fill your heart
so will you be strong in the Lord,
and in the power of His might.

Andrew Murray

When you don't understand what God is doing,
practice being quiet.

Allen Jackson

God is God. He knows what he is doing.
When you can't trace his hand, trust his heart.

Max Lucado

By ourselves we are not capable of suffering bravely,
but the Lord possesses all the strength we lack
and will demonstrate His power when
we undergo persecution.

Corrie ten Boom

And in truth, if we only knew it, our chief fitness is
our utter helplessness. His strength is made perfect,
not in our strength, but in our weakness.
Our strength is only a hindrance.

Hannah Whitall Smith

God's promises are medicine for the broken heart.
Let Him comfort you. And, after He has comforted
you, try to share that comfort with somebody else.
It will do both of you good.

Warren Wiersbe

Date:_____

Let's Give Thanks: Today I am thankful for . . .

_____

_____

_____

_____

_____

Let's Trust God: Today I will lay aside my worries and anxieties regarding . . .

_____

_____

_____

_____

Let's Pray: Today I will pray for . . .

_____

_____

_____

_____

_____

_____

CHAPTER 26

WELCOME THE HOLY SPIRIT

Heavenly Father, I welcome Your Holy Spirit into my life—without any resistance. I need Your help. Apart from You I cannot stand. Thank You for Your abiding presence, Your great power, and Your mercy. Give me an understanding heart that I may serve the living God with joy and freedom. May Your life strengthen me today—body, soul, and spirit. In Jesus' name, amen.

JOHN 16:13

But when he, the Spirit of truth, comes, he will guide you into all truth.

TODAY'S THOUGHTS ABOUT
THE HOLY SPIRIT

The Holy Spirit is the divine substitute
on earth today for the bodily presence
of the Lord Jesus Christ two thousand years ago.

Alan Redpath

If only we would stop lamenting and look up,
God is here. Christ is risen.
The Spirit has been poured out from on high.

A. W. Tozer

The church needs the power and the gifts
of the Holy Spirit more now than ever before.

Corrie ten Boom

The Lord Jesus by His Holy Spirit is with me,
and the knowledge of His presence dispels
the darkness and allays any fears.

Bill Bright

Father, for this day, renew within me
the gift of the Holy Spirit.

Andrew Murray

The Holy Spirit is given to every believer,
not for a limited time, but forever.

Billy Graham

Peace and freedom from fear are linked to
our cooperation with the person of the Holy Spirit.

Allen Jackson

The weakness of our faith is ours,
but the strength of our faith
comes from the Holy Spirit.

C. H. Spurgeon

The joy of the Holy Spirit is experienced
by giving thanks in all situations.

Bill Bright

Date:_____

Let's Give Thanks: Today I am thankful for . . .

_____

_____

_____

_____

_____

Let's Trust God: Today I will lay aside my worries
and anxieties regarding . . .

_____

_____

_____

_____

Let's Pray: Today I will pray for . . .

_____

_____

_____

_____

_____

_____

CHAPTER 27

CULTIVATING STRONG HOPE

Heavenly Father, I thank You for the hope You provided in Christ Jesus. I choose to put on the helmet of salvation and may Your "living hope" protect my thoughts and my emotions. I lift my voice and my eyes to You today. I choose to fix my thoughts and attention on the majesty and power of my God. I give You glory and honor and praise. May Your hope flow through my life this week. In Jesus name, amen.

ROMANS 15:13

May the God of hope fill you with all joy and peace as you trust in him, so that you may overflow with hope by the power of the Holy Spirit.

TODAY'S THOUGHTS ABOUT HOPE

The earth's troubles fade in
the light of heaven's hope.

Billy Graham

Faith is the Christian's foundation,
hope is his anchor, death is his harbor,
Christ is his pilot, and heaven is his country.

Jeremy Taylor

Jesus gives us hope because He keeps us company,
has a vision and knows the way we should go.

Max Lucado

The Bible is a book of tremendous hope.

Allen Jackson

'Tis always morning somewhere.

Henry Wadsworth Longfellow

Take courage. We walk in the wilderness today
and in the Promised Land tomorrow.

D. L. Moody

At least ten times every day, affirm this thought:
"I expect the best and, with God's help,
I will attain the best."

Norman Vincent Peale

Positive minds full of faith and hope
produce positive lives.

Joyce Meyer

Consider the work of Calvary.
A perfect work, perfect in every respect,
perfect in every aspect.

Derek Prince

We never get anywhere—nor
do our conditions and circumstances change—
when we look at the dark side of life.

Mrs. Charles E. Cowman

Date:_____

Let's Give Thanks: Today I am thankful for . . .

_____

_____

_____

_____

_____

Let's Trust God: Today I will lay aside my worries and anxieties regarding . . .

_____

_____

_____

_____

Let's Pray: Today I will pray for . . .

_____

_____

_____

_____

_____

CHAPTER 28

POWER OF GOD

Heavenly Father, may Your glory be manifest in our midst; in the midst of our children, our worship—throughout our community. Let the power of God be made evident. Give us understanding hearts to know the mind of God. May a spirit of repentance and the fear of the Lord grow within us. Holy Spirit, grant us a revelation of Jesus that will bring strength, wholeness, and freedom. In all these things may Jesus be exalted, amen.

ROMANS 1:16–17

I am not ashamed of the gospel, because it is the power of God for the salvation of everyone who believes: first for the Jew, then for the Gentile. For in the gospel a righteousness from God is revealed, a righteousness that is by faith from first to last, just as it is written: "The righteous will live by faith."

TODAY'S THOUGHTS ABOUT GOD'S POWER

Let God's promises shine on your problems.

Corrie ten Boom

He has transforming power. He can change the quality of our lives.

Charles Swindoll

Lord, what joy to know that Your powers are so much greater than those of the enemy.

Corrie ten Boom

What we are powerless to do in our own lives, Christ was powerful enough to accomplish for everyone who would believe.

Bill Hybels

God is able to do what we can't do.

Billy Graham

We have to pray with our eyes on God,
not on the difficulties.

Oswald Chambers

There is no limit to God. There is no limit
to His power. There is no limit to His love.
There is no limit to His mercy.

Billy Graham

Throughout history, when God's people found
themselves facing impossible odds, they reminded
themselves of God's limitless power.

Bill Hybels

The Church is a declaration throughout the earth
of the grace and the power of Almighty God.

Allen Jackson

Let God's promises shine on your problems.

Corrie ten Boom

Date:_____

Let's Give Thanks: Today I am thankful for . . .

_____

_____

_____

_____

_____

Let's Trust God: Today I will lay aside my worries and anxieties regarding . . .

_____

_____

_____

_____

Let's Pray: Today I will pray for . . .

_____

_____

_____

_____

_____

CHAPTER 29

NO WORRIES

Heavenly Father, I rejoice in Your provision for my life. Today I choose to lay aside anxiety and worry. I repent of ignoring Your direction. My future is secure in You and Your great provision for my life. I will lift up my eyes to my King and my Redeemer. You are my help and my provision. You are my sustainer and my deliverer. You are my strength and my exceedingly great reward. Let the name of Jesus be exalted throughout the earth. In His name I pray, amen.

PHILIPPIANS 4:5–6

Let your gentleness be evident to all. The Lord is near. Do not be anxious about anything, but in everything, by prayer and petition, with thanksgiving, present your requests to God.

TODAY'S THOUGHTS ABOUT OVERCOMING WORRY

Anxiety is not only a pain which we must
ask God to assuage but also a weakness
we must ask him to pardon, for he's told us
to take no care for the morrow.

C. S. Lewis

Worry and anxiety are sand in
the machinery of life; faith is the oil.

E. Stanley Jones

Worry is the antithesis of trust.
You simply cannot do both.
They are mutually exclusive.

Elisabeth Elliot

Christ's protest is not against work,
but against anxious thought.

Henry Drummond

The beginning of anxiety is the end of faith,
and the beginning of true faith is the end of anxiety.

George Mueller

To move beyond worry is to press into life
with a renewed vision of who God is,
and with a recognition of His strength
and provision in our lives.

Allen Jackson

No man ever sank under the burden of the day.
It is when tomorrow's burden is added
to the burden of today that the weight is more
than a man can bear. Never load yourself so.

George MacDonald

Knowing that God is faithful,
it really helps me to not be captivated by worry.

Josh McDowell

God is and all is well.

John Greenleaf Whittier

Date:_____

Let's Give Thanks: Today I am thankful for . . .

_____

_____

_____

_____

_____

Let's Trust God: Today I will lay aside my worries
and anxieties regarding . . .

_____

_____

_____

_____

Let's Pray: Today I will pray for . . .

_____

_____

_____

_____

_____

_____

CHAPTER 30

THE APOSTLES' CREED

I believe in God the Father Almighty, maker of heaven and earth. And in Jesus Christ His only Son, our Lord; who was conceived by the Holy Spirit, born of the virgin Mary, suffered under Pontius Pilate, was crucified, dead, and buried. He descended into hades; the third day He rose again from the dead: He ascended into heaven, and sits on the right hand of God, the Father Almighty; from thence He shall come to judge the living and the dead. I believe in the Holy Spirit, the holy Christian church, the communion of saints, the forgiveness of sins, the resurrection of the body, and the life everlasting. Amen.

I WILL NOT STOP

God has uniquely blessed us—
    the best is yet to come.
God has heard our prayers.
God has healed our bodies.
God has restored our marriages.
God has protected our children.
God has delivered us from oppression.

We live in a season of shaking.
    God is shaking the earth.
He is restoring the Jewish people
    and purifying His Church.
If we look at the things which can be shaken
    we will be filled with terror.
If we look at the eternal Kingdom of our Lord,
    we will be filled with anticipation.

Our determination as we gather today is to declare
    before one another and Almighty God—
We are not satisfied. We are not distracted.
We are not weary in doing good.
    We are not discouraged.
We have our eyes on the cross
    and our hearts set on the prize.
We believe the One who has
    promised is Faithful.
We believe the Holy Spirit is our Helper.

We believe that what we ask in Jesus' name
　　　our Father provides.
We believe that the King of kings is returning
　　　to the earth in all of His glory—and we
　　　intend to be about His business until that
　　　moment in time.

We have cast our lot with the Prince of Peace.
We have yielded our will to the Lord of lords.
We are servants of the King.
We reflect the beauty of the Lily of the Valley,
We stand in the strength of the Lion of Judah.
We live in health through the Great Physician.
Our needs are met because He is our Abundance.
We know our path because we follow
　　　the Great Shepherd.
We are participants in the Kingdom of God
　　　because we found THE Door.

We are righteous because of His Sacrifice.
We have taken hold of true life because He is risen.
His name is Jesus of Nazareth,
He is Christ, our Lord and our King.

We believe The Church is His Body.
We have been commissioned by the King.
Our presence on Planet Earth is ordained
　　　by Almighty God.
We are empowered by the Spirit of the Living God.

The angels are ministering Spirits sent forth on
our behalf.
Our reward is sure. Our inheritance is unfading.
Our treasure is secure—it will not diminish.
Our role is pivotal. Our faithfulness is required.
Together we stand, united in heart and purpose
to accomplish the purposes of God in our
generation.

We know not all will go with us.
We recognize the journey is long, there is a
price to pay.
We are aware of an adversary.
We wrestle with the inconsistency of our own hearts.
We see many temptations.
We weep for the pain and suffering around us.

Our plans are made. Our course is charted.
Our heart is fixed. The One who promised is Faithful.
The one who called us will deliver us to our
destination.
The author of our faith is also the completer
of our story.
His strength is sufficient.
His wisdom is transcendent.
His watchfulness is flawless.
His presence is permanent.
His joy is our strength.

CONCLUSION

This book is intended to provide a daily reminder that we are not alone; God is watching over our lives. Jesus makes the Almighty God a very personal part of our journey. He is our High Priest, interceding for us.

There is great hope in knowing that Jesus is our advocate. Continue to offer these prayers to God because the practice of prayer opens doors of possibility. The God who parted the Red Sea, delivered Daniel from a den of lions, and walked on the Sea of Galilee is still at work in the earth. He cares for you! Take your prayers boldly before the throne of grace.

HEBREWS 4:14-16

Therefore, since we have a great high priest who has gone through the heavens, Jesus the Son of God, let us hold firmly to the faith we profess. For we do not have a high priest who is unable to sympathize with our weaknesses, but we have one who has been tempted in every way, just as we are—yet was without sin. Let us then approach the throne of grace with confidence, so that we may receive mercy and find grace to help us in our time of need.

ABOUT THE AUTHOR

G. Allen Jackson is passionate about helping people become fully devoted followers of Jesus Christ who "respond to God's invitations for their life."

He has served World Outreach Church in Murfreesboro, Tennessee, as senior pastor since 1989. Under his leadership, the fellowship has grown to a congregation of over 10,000 that reaches many thousands more with the Gospel through community events and worship services.

Pastor Jackson's challenging messages are broadcast via television to over 25 million households and stream over the Internet to 139 countries. He has spoken at pastors' conferences in the U.S. and abroad, and for many years has been a featured speaker at the International Christian Embassy Jerusalem's Feast of Tabernacles celebration. Through Intend Ministries, Jackson coaches pastors around the world and publishes small-group curriculum used in 34 states as well as Israel, Guatemala, the Philippines, Bermuda, Mexico, and South Africa.

With degrees from Oral Roberts University and Vanderbilt University, and additional studies at Gordon-Conwell Theological Seminary and Hebrew University of Jerusalem, Jackson is uniquely equipped to help people develop a love and understanding of God's Word. Pastor Jackson's wife, Kathy, is an active participant in ministry at World Outreach Church.